THE **TESTING** SERIES

PRISON OFFICER
TESTS

THE **TESTING** SERIES
expert advice on interview preparation

how2become

Orders: Please contact How2become Ltd,
Suite 2, 50 Churchill Square Business Centre, Kings Hill, Kent ME19 4YU.

You can order via the email address info@how2become.co.uk or through our
UK distributor Gardners books at Gardners.com.

ISBN: 9781907558887

First published 2012

Typeset for How2become Ltd by Molly Hill, Canada.

Printed in Great Britain for How2become Ltd by: CMP (uk) Limited, Poole, Dorset.

CONTENTS

INTRODUCTION   **V**

CHAPTER 1
THE PRISON OFFICER SELECTION TEST   **1**

CHAPTER 2
MOCK EXAM 1   **5**

CHAPTER 3
MOCK EXAM 2   **21**

CHAPTER 4
MOCK EXAM 3   **33**

CHAPTER 5
MOCK EXAM 4   **49**

CHAPTER 6
RECALLING VISUAL INFORMATION TESTS   **63**

CHAPTER 7
READING COMPREHENSION EXERCISES   **79**

INTRODUCTION

Dear Sir/Madam,

Welcome to your new guide: Prison Officer Tests. This guide has been designed to help you prepare for and pass the Prison Officer Selection Tests, or POST as they are otherwise called. You will find the guide both a comprehensive and highly informative tool for helping you obtain one of the most sought after careers available.

The job of a Prison Officer is both highly challenging and rewarding. You will need a certain set of special skills in order to carry out the role competently. As you can imagine, at times you could be dealing with some of the country's most notorious prisoner's. Being a Prison Officer is not about punishing or bullying inmates. It is about treating them correctly and rehabilitating them, ready for when they eventually return to society. This guide has been specifically created to focus on the selection tests that are required to pass the selection process. Part of the role of a Prison Officer requires an ability to use and interpret numerical data accurately. You will find that within the guide many of the questions are based around a requirement to carry out basic numerical equation, such as addition and subtraction. Accuracy is crucial if you are to gain sufficient scores in the tests. Another key element to the tests is your ability to accurately check, and cross-check, supplied information. Let us assume that you are responsible for a specific section of a prison. You will be required to count the number of prisoners there are in your specific area and report any discrepancies immediately. Your ability to carry out accurate assessments is essential to the role.

I believe that I have provided you with sufficient sample test questions to help you prepare. However, if you would like any further assistance with the selection process then we offer the following products and training courses via the website **www.how2become.co.uk**:

- How to pass the Prison Officer Selection Test Role-Play DVD
- Prison Officer Selection Test (POST) online testing facility;
- One-Day Prison Officer training course.

Finally, you won't achieve much in life without hard work, determination and perseverance. Work hard, stay focused and be what you want!

Good luck and best wishes,

Richard McMunn
Managing Director and Founder
How2Become.co.uk

CHAPTER 1
THE PRISON OFFICER SELECTION TEST

Once you have made your initial online application, and it has been successful, you will be invited to sit an online Prison Officer Selection Test (POST). The test itself is designed to be representative of the types of numerical tasks that Prison Officers are required to carry out on a daily basis.

There are four sections to the test consisting of a total of 56 questions. You have 60 minutes to complete the test, which equates to approximately 15 minutes per section. It is very important that you are the person who actually carries out the test, as there is a similar version of the POST to be undertaken at the Recruitment Assessment Day.

The good news is you are permitted to use a calculator and you do not lose any marks for incorrect answers. The questions that you will face during the online POST are predominantly based around numerical reasoning and include:

• Addition, subtraction, multiplication and division

• Ratios and percentages

• Cross referencing lists and checking information

- Interpreting graphs and charts
- The use of the 24-hour clock

Jobs of this nature require you to be competent in the use of the 24-hour clock. During the Prison Officer Selection Test (POST) you will be required to answer a number of questions that are based around the use of the 24-hour clock. There are effectively two ways to show the time: "AM/PM" or "24-hour clock":

> With the 24-Hour Clock the time is shown as how many hours and minutes have passed since midnight.

> With AM/PM (or the "12-Hour Clock") the day is split into the 12 hours running from midnight to noon (the AM hours) and the other 12 hours running from noon to midnight (the PM hours).

CONVERTING AM/PM TO 24-HOUR CLOCK

For the first hour of the day (12 midnight to 12:59 AM), subtract 12 hours.
Examples: 12 midnight = 0:00, 12:35 AM = 0:35

From 1:00 AM to 12:59 PM, no change
Examples: 11:20 AM = 11:20, 12:30 PM = 12:30

From 1:00 PM to 11:59 PM, add 12 hours
Examples: 4:45 PM = 16:45, 11:50 PM = 23:50

CONVERTING 24-HOUR CLOCK TO AM/PM

For the first hour of the day (0:00 to 0:59), add 12 hours, make it "AM"
Examples: 0:10 = 12:10 AM, 0:40 = 12:40 AM

From 1:00 to 11:59, just make it "AM"
Examples: 1:15 = 1:15 AM, 11:25 = 11:25 AM

From 12:00 to 12:59, just make it "PM"
Examples: 12:10 = 12:10 PM, 12:55 = 12:55 PM

From 13:00 to 23:59, subtract 12 hours and make it "PM"
Examples: 14:55 = 2:55 PM, 23:30 = 11:30 PM

CONVERSION CHART

Here is a side-by-side comparison of the 24-hour clock and AM/PM:

0:00	12:00 Midnight
01:00	1:00 AM
02:00	2:00 AM
03:00	3:00 AM
04:00	4:00 AM
05:00	5:00 AM
06:00	6:00 AM
07:00	7:00 AM
08:00	8:00 AM
09:00	9:00 AM
10:00	10:00 AM
11:00	11:00 AM
12:00	12:00 Noon
13:00	1:00 PM
14:00	2:00 PM
15:00	3:00 PM
16:00	4:00 PM
17:00	5:00 PM
18:00	6:00 PM
19:00	7:00 PM
20:00	8:00 PM
21:00	9:00 PM
22:00	10:00 PM
23:00	11:00 PM

Before you sit the online version of the Prison Officer Selection Test, make sure you are competent in the use of the 24-hour clock.

Once you have successfully passed the online POST you will be invited to attend a Recruitment Assessment Day. During the Recruitment Assessment Day you will sit a language test. This test assesses you against:

- Listening, taking notes and recalling heard information – You will listen to an oral briefing about events in a prison. You will be advised to take notes on rough paper provided. On completion of the briefing you will be asked to write down answers to questions relating to the information you have just heard.

- Completing a standard form – You will complete a standard form using written information provided about a prisoner.

- Checking information for discrepancies, errors and omissions – You will compare two lists and identify discrepancies and/or omissions on the second list.

- Applying rules – You will be presented with two lists; the first shows cells where prisoners belong (sleep) on a prison wing; the second shows where they are currently located on the wing. You will compare the information on these two lists, and apply three rules in order to determine if everyone is present on the wing and who (if anyone) is breaking the rules.

- Reading comprehension – You will read text extracted from a standard Prison Service source (e.g. Prison Service Orders, intranet, manuals etc) and then answer questions about the text.

- Recalling visual (seen) information from memory – You will be shown a colour photograph of a prison scene for three minutes. The photograph is removed and you will be asked several questions about what you saw. Note taking is not permitted on this exercise.

Over the next few pages I have provided you with a number of mock exams that will go a long way to helping you prepare effectively. The questions contained within the tests are similar to the types you will encounter during the online POST and also the POST at the Recruitment Assessment Day.

Once you have completed each test, take the time to check your answers thoroughly.

CHAPTER 2
MOCK EXAM 1

PRISON OFFICER SELECTION TEST MOCK EXAMS

In mock exam 1 there are 50 questions and you will have a maximum of 50 minutes to complete them. You can use rough paper to work your answers out.

We recommend that you use a calculator to help you answer some of the questions. Make sure that you are comfortable and in an area where you will not be distracted.

All the questions in this test are designed to be representative of the types of numerical tasks that prison officers are required to carry out on a daily basis.

It is important that you are the one that completes this test as there is an element of retest in the next part of the selection process at the assessment day.

You will not lose marks for incorrect questions.

Good Luck!

MOCK EXAM 1

Use the diagram to answer the questions.

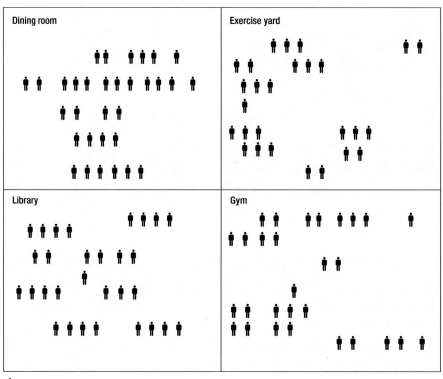

 = 1 prisoner

Q1. Which area has the most prisoners?

Answer:

Q2. Which area has the least prisoners?

Answer:

Q3. How many prisoners are in the dining room?

Answer:

Q4. How many prisoners are in the exercise yard?

Answer: [   ]

Q5. How many prisoners are in the library?

Answer: [   ]

Q6. How many prisoners are in the gym?

Answer: [   ]

Q7. A quarter of all prisoners in the dining room go to the gym.
How many prisoners remain in the dining room?

Answer: [   ]

Q8. Half the prisoners in the library go to the dining room.
How many prisoners remain in the library?

Answer: [   ]

Q9. One third of the prisoners in the exercise yard go to the dining room.
How many prisoners remain in the exercise yard?

Answer: [   ]

Q10. In total there are 110 prisoners living on wing one, 10 prison officers
are on duty. What is the ratio of prisoners to prison officers?

Answer: [   ]

Use the diagram to answer the questions.

Kitchen

Gymnasium

TV room

Educational block

● = 1 prisoner

Q11. How many prisoners are there in total?

Answer:

Q12. How many more prisoners are there in the TV room than in the Educational block?

Answer:

Q13. If 50% of prisoners in the Gymnasium and 6 prisoners from the Kitchen move to the Educational block, how many prisoners will be in the Educational block?

Answer:

Q14. If the number of prisoners in the Educational block tripled, how many prisoners would there be in total in the Educational block?

Answer:

Q15. If a third of prisoners in the Educational block and 20% of prisoners in the Gymnasium move to the Kitchen, how many prisoners will there be in the Kitchen?

Answer:

Use the diagram to answer the questions.

● = 1 prisoner

Q16. How many prisoners are there in total?

Answer:

Q17. How many more prisoners are there in the Visitors room than in the Educational block?

Answer:

Q18. If half of the prisoners in the Visitors room move to the Gymnasium, how many prisoners will there now be in the Gymnasium?

Answer:

Q19. If 25% of prisoners in the Visitors room and 25% of prisoners in the Gymnasium leave the prison altogether how many prisoners will there be left?

Answer:

Q20. If the maximum number of prisoners that a prison officer can supervise at any one time is 5, how many prison officers should be in attendance in the Visitors room?

Answer:

Use the diagram to answer the questions.

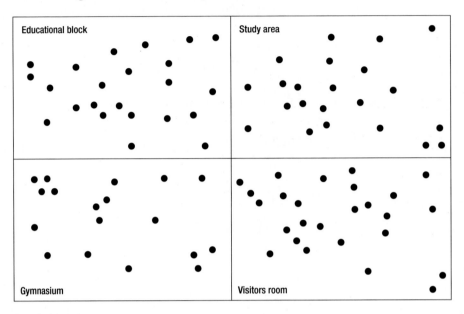

● = 1 prisoner

Q21. How many prisoners are there in the Visitors room?

Answer:

Q22. How many prisoners are there in the Gymnasium?

Answer:

Q23. If 50% of prisoners from the Study room and 50% of prisoners from the Visitors room move to the Educational block, how many prisoners will there be in the Educational block?

Answer:

Q24. Which area has the most prisoners?

Answer:

Q25. Which area has the least prisoners?

Answer:

Q26. If 7 prisoners leave from each area how many prisoners will there be in total?

Answer:

Use the diagram to answer the questions.

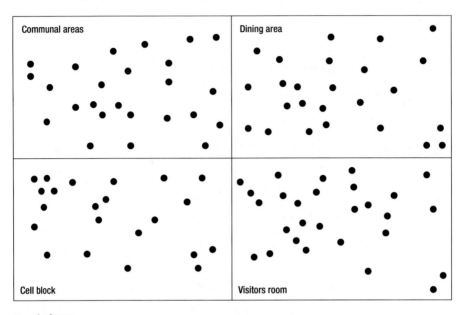

● = 1 prisoner

Q27. Which area has the most prisoners?

Answer:

Q28. Which area has the least prisoners?

Answer:

Q29. How many prisoners are there in total?

Answer:

Q30. If half of the prisoners in the Cells and half of the prisoners in the Visiting room move to the Communal areas, how many prisoners will there be in the Communal areas?

Answer: [   ]

Q31. If the ratio of prisoners to prison officers is 10:1 how many prison officers will there be?

Answer: [   ]

Q32. If the ratio of prisoners to prison officers is 10:1 how many prison officers will there be?

Answer: [   ]

Q33. If the ratio of prisoners to prison officers in the Communal areas is 5:1 how many prison officers will there be?

Answer: [   ]

Q34. How many prisoners are there in the Dining room and the Visiting room?

Answer: [   ]

Use the diagram to answer the questions.

Cell block 1

Cell block 2

Cell block 5

Cell block 7

Cell block 4

Cell block 3

Cell block 8

Cell block 6

● = 1 prisoner

Q35. 3 prisoners from Cell block 3 go to the Gymnasium. How many prisoners are left in Cell block 3?

Answer:

Q36. Which block has the least number of prisoners?

Answer:

Q37. How many prisoners are there in total?

Answer:

Q38. How many prisoners are there in Cell blocks 3, 5 and 8?

Answer:

Q39. 25% of all prisoners leave the prison. How many prisoners are left?

Answer: [   ]

Q40. If 30% of prisoners in Cell block 7 move to Cell block 1, how many prisoners will there be in Cell block 7?

Answer: [   ]

Q41. If 30% of prisoners in Cell block 7 move to Cell block 1, how many prisoners will there be in Cell block 1?

Answer: [   ]

Q42. How many prisoners are there in Cell blocks 1, 2, 4 and 6?

Answer: [   ]

Q43. If the ratio of prisoners to prison officers is 10:1 how many prison officers will there be?

Answer: [   ]

Q44. If the ratio of prisoners to prison officers is 25:1 how many prison officers will there be?

Answer: [   ]

Use the diagram to answer the questions.

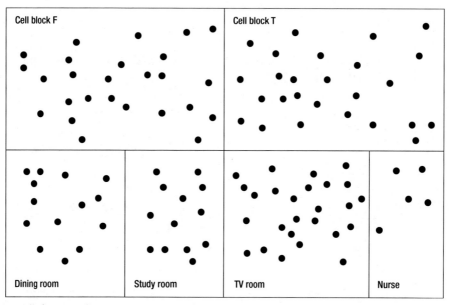

● = 1 prisoner

Q45. How many prisoners are there in total?

Answer: [   ]

Q46. If 50% of prisoners move from Cell block F to Cell block T how may prisoners will there be in Cell block T?

Answer: [   ]

Q47. If 50% of prisoners move from Cell block F to Cell block T how may prisoners will there be in Cell block F?

Answer: [   ]

Q48. How many prisoners are not in Cell blocks?

Answer: [   ]

Q49. If the number of prisoners visiting the Nurse increases by 100%, how many people will there be visiting the Nurse?

Answer: [   ]

Q50. How many prisoners are there in Cell blocks?

Answer: [   ]

Now check your answers with the ones that follow before moving on to the next mock exam.

ANSWERS TO MOCK EXAM 1

Q1.	Dining room	**Q26.**	61
Q2.	Exercise yard	**Q27.**	Visitor's room
Q3.	32	**Q28.**	Cells
Q4.	27	**Q29.**	100
Q5.	30	**Q30.**	50
Q6.	29	**Q31.**	20
Q7.	24	**Q32.**	10
Q8.	15	**Q33.**	5
Q9.	18	**Q34.**	53
Q10.	11:1	**Q35.**	8
Q11.	43	**Q36.**	Cell block 6
Q12.	4	**Q37.**	100
Q13.	20	**Q38.**	47
Q14.	27	**Q39.**	75
Q15.	16	**Q40.**	7
Q16.	67	**Q41.**	14
Q17.	6	**Q42.**	43
Q18.	26	**Q43.**	10
Q19.	58	**Q44.**	4
Q20.	4	**Q45.**	110
Q21.	26	**Q46.**	39
Q22.	18	**Q47.**	13
Q23.	47	**Q48.**	58
Q24.	Visitor's room	**Q49.**	10
Q25.	Gymnasium	**Q50.**	52

CHAPTER 3
MOCK EXAM 2

In mock exam 2 there are 50 questions and you will have a maximum of 50 minutes to complete them. You can use rough paper to work your answers out.

We recommend that you use a calculator to help you answer some of the questions. Make sure that you are comfortable and in an area where you will not be distracted.

All the questions in this test are designed to be representative of the types of numerical tasks that prison officers are required to carry out on a daily basis.

It is important that you are the one that completes this test as there is an element of retest in the next part of the selection process at the assessment day.

You will not lose marks for incorrect questions.

Good Luck!

Use the diagram to answer the questions.

Hospital

Visitors centre

Kitchen

Dining room

† = 1 prisoner

Q1. How many prisoners are in the hospital and visitors centre in total?

Answer:

Q2. How many prisoners are in the kitchen and in the dining room in total?

Answer:

Q3. How many more prisoners are in the dining room than the visitors centre?

Answer:

Q4. 50% of the prisoners in the kitchen go for their lunch in the dining room. How many prisoners are now in the dining room?

Answer: [   ]

Q5. 50% of the prisoners in the visitors centre are moved to the hospital. How many prisoners are now in the hospital?

Answer: [   ]

Q6. 39 prisoners live on the red wing. Of these, 12 have gone to gym. How many prisoners remain on the red wing?

Answer: [   ]

Q7. 36 prisoners live on the blue wing. Of these, 5 have gone to the gym and 15 have gone to the exercise yard. How many prisoners remain on the blue wing?

Answer: [   ]

Q8. 84 prisoners live on the yellow wing. Of these, 9 have gone to music group, 8 have gone to see the nurse and 20 have gone to the education centre. How many prisoners have left yellow wing?

Answer: [   ]

Q9. 78 prisoners live on the green wing. Of these, 16 have gone to the shower room, 34 have gone to the dining hall and 10 have gone to the workshop. How many prisoners remain on the green wing?

Answer: [   ]

Q10. 118 prisoners live on the brown wing. Of these, 12 have gone to the shower room, 23 have gone to the dining hall and 11 have gone to the workshop. How many prisoners remain on the brown wing?

Answer: [   ]

Q11. 118 prisoners live on the brown wing. Of these, 12 have gone to the shower room, 23 have gone to the dining hall and 11 have gone to the workshop. How many prisoners have left brown wing?

Answer:

Q12. 281 prisoners live on the blue wing. Of these, 16 have gone to the dining area, 29 have gone to the gymnasium and 14 have gone to the workshop. How many prisoners remain on the blue wing?

Answer:

Q13. 281 prisoners live on the blue wing. Of these, 16 have gone to the dining area, 29 have gone to the gymnasium and 14 have gone to the workshop. How many prisoners have left the blue wing?

Answer:

Use the diagram to answer the questions.

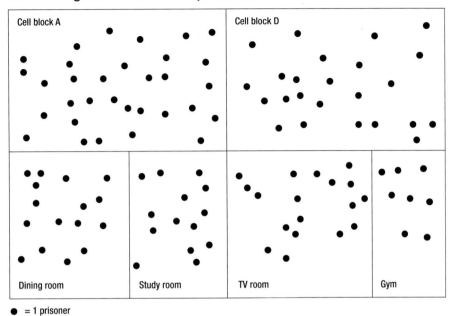

= 1 prisoner

Q14. How many more prisoners are there in the TV room than in the Gym?

Answer:

Q15. If 50% of prisoners move from Cell block D to Cell block A, how many prisoners will there be in Cell block D?

Answer:

Q16. If 50% of prisoners move from Cell block D to Cell block A, how many prisoners will there be in Cell block A?

Answer:

Q17. Which area has the most prisoners?

Answer:

Q18. Which area has the least prisoners?

Answer:

Q19. How many prisoners are there in total?

Answer:

Q20. If the ratio of prisoners to prison officers in the Cell Block A is 8:1, how many prison officers will there be?

Answer:

Q21. There are 144 prisoners in H wing of HMP Fictown. If the ratio of prisoners to prison officers is 12:1, how many prison officers are there?

Answer:

Q22. There are 450 prisoners at HMP Fictown. If the ratio of prisoners to prison officers is 25:1, how many prison officers are there?

Answer:

Q23. There are 480 prisoners at HMP Winderlass. If the ratio of prisoners to prison officers is 40:1, how many prison officers are there?

Answer:

Q24. There are 720 prisoners at HMP Gleaming. If the ratio of prisoners to prison officers is 45:1, how many prison officers are there?

Answer:

Use the diagram to answer the questions.

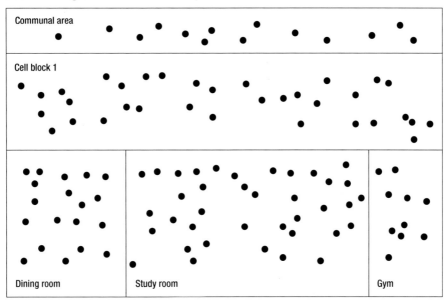

● = 1 prisoner

Q25. Which area has the most prisoners?

Answer:

Q26. Which area has the second least prisoners?

Answer:

Q27. How many prisoners are there in total?

Answer:

Q28. If 50% of prisoners from Cell block 1 and 50% of prisoners from the Study room move to the Communal area, how many prisoners will there be in the Communal area?

Answer:

Q29. If 50% of prisoners from the Gym and 50% of prisoners in the Communal area leave the prison how many prisoners will there be in total?

Answer:

Q30. If the ratio of prisoners to prison officers in the Cell block 1 is 7:1 how many prison officers will there be?

Answer:

Q31. If the ratio of prisoners to prison officers in the Gym is 5:1 how many prison officers will there be?

Answer:

Q32. Which area has the third most prisoners?

Answer:

Q33. If the number of prisoners in the Communal area increased by 50%, how many prisoners would there be in the Communal area?

Answer:

Q34. If the number of prisoners in the Dining room increased by 100%, how many prisoner would there be in the Dining room?

Answer:

Q35. If the number of prisoners in the Cell block 1 increased by 100%, how many prisoners would there be in Cell block 1?

Answer:

Use the diagram to answer the questions.

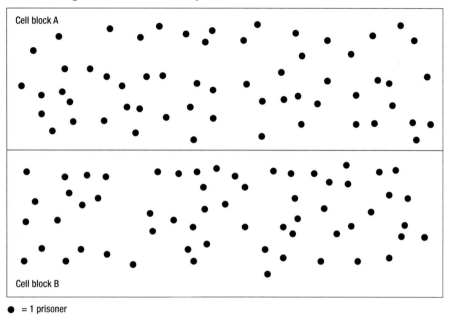

● = 1 prisoner

Q36. Which block has the least prisoners?

Answer:

Q37. How many prisoners are there in total?

Answer:

Q38. If 30% of prisoners leave Cell block B, how many prisoners will there be left in Cell Block B?

Answer:

Q39. If 30% of prisoners leave Cell block B, how many prisoners will there be left in total?

Answer:

Q40. If 60% of prisoners move from Cell block B to Cell block A, how many prisoners will there be in Cell block A?

Answer:

Q41. If 60% of prisoners move from Cell block B to Cell block A, how many prisoners will there be in Cell block B?

Answer:

Q42. If the ratio of prisoners to prison officers in Cell block B is 10:1 how many prison officers will there be?

Answer:

Q43. If the ratio of prisoners to prison officers in Cell block B is 20:1 how many prison officers will there be?

Answer:

Q44. If the ratio of prisoners to prison officers in Cell block B is 5:1 how many prison officers will there be?

Answer:

Q45. If 23 prisoners from Cell block A and 22 prisoners from Cell block B leave the prison, how many prisoners will be left?

Answer:

Q46. If 17 prisoners from Cell block A and 47 prisoners from Cell block B leave the prison, how many prisoners will be left?

Answer:

Q47. If 11 prisoners join Cell block A and 13 prisoners join Cell block B how many prisoners will there be in total?

Answer:

Q48. The maximum number of prisoners permitted in Cell block B is 80. If the number of prisoners in Cell block B increases by 30% from its current total will the maximum number be breached?

Answer:

Q49. The maximum number of prisoners permitted in Cell block B is 95. If the number of prisoners in Cell block B increases by 60% from its current total will the maximum number be breached?

Answer:

Q50. The maximum number of prisoners permitted in Cell block A is 106. If the number of prisoners in Cell block B increases by 80% from its current total will the maximum number be breached?

Answer:

Now check your answers with the ones that follow before moving on to the next mock exam.

ANSWERS TO MOCK EXAM 2

Q1. 95

Q2. 97

Q3. 3

Q4. 74

Q5. 71

Q6. 27

Q7. 16

Q8. 37

Q9. 18

Q10. 72

Q11. 46

Q12. 222

Q13. 59

Q14. 10

Q15. 12

Q16. 44

Q17. Cell block A

Q18. Gym

Q19. 112

Q20 4

Q21. 12

Q22. 18

Q23. 12

Q24. 16

Q25. Study room

Q26. Communal area

Q27. 115

Q28. 50

Q29. 103

Q30. 2

Q31. 2

Q32. Dining room

Q33. 21

Q34. 38

Q35. 68

Q36. Block A

Q37. 119

Q38. 42

Q39. 101

Q40. 95

Q41. 24

Q42. 6

Q43. 3

Q44. 12

Q45. 74

Q46. 55

Q47. 143

Q48. No

Q49. Yes

Q50. No

CHAPTER 4
MOCK EXAM 3

In mock exam 3 there are 50 questions and you will have a maximum of 50 minutes to complete them. You can use rough paper to work your answers out.

We recommend that you use a calculator to help you answer some of the questions. Make sure that you are comfortable and in an area where you will not be distracted.

All the questions in this test are designed to be representative of the types of numerical tasks that prison officers are required to carry out on a daily basis.

It is important that you are the one that completes this test as there is an element of retest in the next part of the selection process at the assessment day.

You will not lose marks for incorrect questions.

Good Luck!

Use the following diagram to answer the questions

	SENTENCE LENGTH	
	SHORT TERM	LONG TERM
Red Wing	80	15
Blue Wing	92	12
Yellow Wing	61	25
Green Wing	84	22
Orange Wing	75	26

Q1. HMP Houghton has 492 prisoners; the sentence breakdown can be seen in the table above. How many short-term prisoners are at HMP Crofton?

Answer:

Q2. HMP Houghton has 492 prisoners; the sentence breakdown can be seen in the table above. How many long-term prisoners are at HMP Crofton?

Answer:

Q3. All short-term and long-term prisoners on the green and orange wings are moved to another prison. How many prisoners remain at HMP Houghton?

Answer:

Q4. 80 prison officers work at HMP Houghton. Of these, 30 work on the red wing, 15 work on the blue wing and 15 work on the green wing. Of the remaining prison officers 50% work on the yellow wing and 50% work on the orange wing. How many prison officers work on the yellow wing?

Answer:

Q5. There are 36 cells on the red wing. Each cell has two beds. How many beds are there on the red wing?

Answer:

Q6. There are 25 tables in the dining hall. Of these, 15 tables have 11 chairs each and 10 tables have 25 chairs each. How many chairs are there in the dining hall?

Answer:

Q7. At HMP Houghton prisoners earn 90 pence a day for working in the textile workshop. How much would a prisoner earn if they worked for 3 days?

Answer:

Q8. At HMP Houghton prisoners can earn £1.40 a day for working in the kitchen. How much would a prisoner earn if they worked for 6 days?

Answer:

Q9. A prisoner works in the library. He works 2.5 hours every morning and 3.5 hours every afternoon for five days a week. How many hours does he work in two weeks?

Answer:

Use the following diagram to answer the questions

ITEM	PRICE	QUANTITY
Milky Bar	£0.35	5
Lotion	£0.52	4
Soap	£0.10	8
		Total

Q10. A prisoner has asked for some help in completing an order form. They have asked for help in calculating the cost of some items. According to the table, how much is spent on Milky Bar?

Answer:

Q11. A prisoner has asked for some help in completing an order form. They have asked for help in calculating the cost of some items. According to the table, how much is spent on Lotion?

Answer:

Q12. A prisoner has asked for some help in completing an order form. They have asked for help in calculating the cost of some items. According to the table, how much is spent on Soap?

Answer:

Q13. A prisoner has asked for some help in completing an order form. They have asked for help in calculating the cost of some items. According to the table, how much is spent on Milky Bar, Lotion and Soap?

Answer:

Q14. A prison officer has been asked to distribute boxes of soap between three wings. There are 54 boxes of soap. If the boxes are shared equally between three wings, how many boxes will each wing have?

Answer:

Q15. It takes a prison officer 20 minutes to search one cell. What is the maximum number of cells a prison officer will be able to search in 3 hours and 20 minutes?

Answer:

Q16. In education it takes a teacher 10 minutes to mark each prisoner's piece of coursework. The teacher has 63 pieces of coursework to mark in total and has allocated 1 hour and 30 minutes each day to mark. How many days will it take the teacher to mark all 63 pieces of coursework?

Answer:

Q17. When prison officers write reports they use the 24 hour clock (e.g. 2:45 pm = 14:45; 9:45 am = 09:45).

Convert 6:30am into 24 hour clock

Answer:

Q18. When prison officers write reports they use the 24 hour clock (e.g. 2:45 pm = 14:45; 9:45 am = 09:45).

Convert 6:30 pm into 24 hour clock.

Answer:

Q19. When prison officers write reports they use the 24 hour clock (e.g. 2:45 pm = 14:45; 9:45 am = 09:45).

Convert 3:00 am into 24 hour clock.

Answer:

Q20. 39 When prison officers write reports they use the 24 hour clock (e.g. 2:45 pm = 14:45; 9:45 am = 09:45).

Convert 12:15 am into 24 hour clock.

Answer:

Q21. When prison officers write reports they use the 24 hour clock (e.g. 2:45 pm = 14:45; 9:45 am = 09:45).

Convert 12:15 pm into 24 hour clock.

Answer:

Q22. A prison officer has a 45 minute lunch break. He leaves the office at 12:45 hours. What time must he return to the office (Please use 24 hour clock)?

Answer:

Q23. 42 HMP Houghton operates the following timetable:

- 08:00 hrs Cells unlocked
- 12:00 hrs Cells locked
- 14:00 hrs Cells unlocked
- 17:30 hrs Cells locked
- 18:30 hrs Cells unlocked
- 21:00 hrs Cells locked

How many hours each day are the cells unlocked?

Answer:

Q24. A prison officer lives in Monks Cross and works at HMP Crofton.

	MONKS CROSS	CANNON HILL	CROFTON ROAD
Bus A	07:15	07:30	07:40
Bus B	07:30	07:45	07:55
Bus C	07:45	08:00	08:10
Bus D	08:00	08:15	08:25

They must be at work by 08:10 hours. Crofton Road bus stop is 5 minutes' walk from HMP Crofton. Use the bus timetable to work out which is the latest bus the prison officer can take to arrive at work on time.

Answer:

Use the graph to answer the questions

Drug Tests at HMP Cannon Farms September 2007

Q25. How many drug tests were carried out in total?

Answer:

Q26. On which wing were the most drug tests conducted in total?

Answer:

Q27. How many negative drug test results were found at HMP Cannon Farms in September 2007?

Answer:

Use the graph to answer the following questions

Prisoner Specialist Dietary Requirements at HMP Cannon Farms

Q28. Which wing has the least prisoners with a vegetarian dietary requirement?

Answer:

Q29. Which wing has more prisoners requiring a vegan diet than a vegetarian diet?

Answer:

Q30. How many more prisoners require a vegetarian diet than a gluten free diet?

Answer:

Q31. 400 staff work at HMP Bornfield. Of these, 300 are female and 100 are male. What percentage of staff are female?

Answer:

Q32. There are 500 prisoners at HMP Townside. Of these, 100 are life sentenced prisoners, 200 are remand prisoners, 125 are sex offenders and

The remainder of prisoners fall within other categories. How many prisoners fall in other categories?

Answer:

Q33. There are 400 prisoners at HMP Canning Town. Of these, 95 are life sentenced prisoners, 200 are remand prisoners, 25 are sex offenders and 80 prisoners fall within other categories. What percentage of prisoners fall within other categories?

Answer:

Q34. 300 prisoners take part in a sporting event. Of these:

    40 do the 100 metre sprint

    30 do the long jump

    50 do the 200 metre sprint

    90 do the high jump

    60 do the 1500 metre race

    30 do the 400 metre hurdles.

What percentage of prisoners take part in the high jump?

Answer:

Q35. A prison officer has been asked to check some prisoner mail, they have been asked to check a random 20% of letters. There are 180 letters in total.

How many letters does the prison officer have to check?

Answer:

Q36. A prisoner is sick. A prison officer is keeping the prisoner under close observation and must check they are ok every 12 minutes. How many checks will the prison officer need to carry out over an 8 hour period?

Answer:

Q37. 70 visitors arrive at HMP Cannon Farms. A prison officer must search 30% of the visitors. Each search takes 4 minutes to carry out. How many minutes will it take the prison officer to carry out the required amount of searches?

Answer:

Q38. When prison officers write reports they use the 24 hour clock (e.g. 2:45 pm = 14:45; 9:45 am = 09:45).

Convert 3.24pm into 24 hour clock

Answer:

Q39. When prison officers write reports they use the 24 hour clock (e.g. 2:45 pm = 14:45; 9:45 am = 09:45).

Convert 8:12 am into 24 hour clock.

Answer:

Q40. When prison officers write reports they use the 24 hour clock (e.g. 2:45 pm = 14:45; 9:45 am = 09:45).

Convert 1:01 am into 24 hour clock.

Answer:

Q41. 39 When prison officers write reports they use the 24 hour clock (e.g. 2:45 pm = 14:45; 9:45 am = 09:45).

Convert 2:11 pm into 24 hour clock.

Answer:

Q42. When prison officers write reports they use the 24 hour clock (e.g. 2:45 pm = 14:45; 9:45 am = 09:45).

Convert 4:44 pm into 24 hour clock.

Answer:

Q43. HMP Ringtown operates the following timetable:

- 08:15 hrs Cells unlocked
- 10:00 hrs Cells locked
- 11:30 hrs Cells unlocked
- 13:30 hrs Cells locked
- 17:30 hrs Cells unlocked
- 21:30 hrs Cells locked

How many hours each day are the cells locked?

Answer:

Q44. HMP Huttonshire operates the following timetable:

- 07:00 hrs Cells unlocked
- 11:00 hrs Cells locked
- 13:00 hrs Cells unlocked
- 18:30 hrs Cells locked
- 19:30 hrs Cells unlocked
- 22:00 hrs Cells locked

How many hours each day are the cells locked?

Answer:

Q45. 300 prisoners take part in a sporting event. Of these:

　10 do the 100 metre sprint

　60 do the long jump

　60 do the 200 metre sprint

　80 do the high jump

　70 do the 1500 metre race

　20 do the 400 metre hurdles.

What percentage of prisoners take part in the long jump?

Answer:

Q46. 300 prisoners take part in a sporting event. Of these:

　10 do the 100 metre sprint

　60 do the long jump

　60 do the 200 metre sprint

　80 do the high jump

　70 do the 1500 metre race

　20 do the 400 metre hurdles.

If 10% of prisoners leave the 400 metres hurdles to take part in the long jump, how many prisoners will there be now taking part in the long jump?

Answer:

Q47. 300 prisoners take part in a sporting event. Of these:

　10 do the 100 metre sprint

　60 do the long jump

　60 do the 200 metre sprint

　80 do the high jump

　70 do the 1500 metre race

　20 do the 400 metre hurdles.

If 20% of prisoners leave the 200 metre sprint to take part in the high jump, how many prisoners will there be now taking part in the high jump?

Answer:

Q48. 400 prisoners take part in a sporting event. Of these:

   60 do the 100 metre sprint

   60 do the long jump

   60 do the 200 metre sprint

   80 do the high jump

   70 do the 1500 metre race

   70 do the 400 metre hurdles.

If 10% of prisoners leave the 400 metre hurdles to take part in the high jump, how many prisoners will there be now taking part in the 400 metre hurdles?

Answer:

Q49. 400 prisoners take part in a sporting event. Of these:

   60 do the 100 metre sprint

   60 do the long jump

   60 do the 200 metre sprint

   80 do the high jump

   70 do the 1500 metre race

   70 do the 400 metre hurdles.

If 30% of prisoners leave the high jump to take part in the long jump, how many prisoners will there be now taking part in the high jump?

Answer:

Q50. 400 prisoners take part in a sporting event. Of these:

   60 do the 100 metre sprint

   60 do the long jump

   60 do the 200 metre sprint

80 do the high jump

70 do the 1500 metre race

70 do the 400 metre hurdles.

If 30% of prisoners leave the high jump to take part in the long jump, how many prisoners will there be now taking part in the long jump?

Answer:

Now check your answers with the ones that follow before moving on to the next section of the guide.

ANSWERS TO MOCK EXAM 3

Q1. 392		**Q26.** Green	
Q2. 100		**Q27.** 70	
Q3. 285		**Q28.** Red	
Q4. 10		**Q29.** Red	
Q5. 72		**Q30.** 75	
Q6. 415		**Q31.** 75%	
Q7. £2.70		**Q32.** 75	
Q8. £8.40		**Q33.** 20%	
Q9. 60 hours		**Q34.** 30%	
Q10. £1.75		**Q35.** 36 letters	
Q11. £2.08		**Q36.** 40 checks	
Q12. £0.80		**Q37.** 84 minutes	
Q13. £4.63		**Q38.** 1524	
Q14. 18 boxes		**Q39.** 0812	
Q15. 10 cells		**Q40.** 0101	
Q16. 7 days		**Q41.** 1411	
Q17. 0630		**Q42.** 1644	
Q18. 1830		**Q43.** 16 hours and 15 minutes	
Q19. 0300		**Q44.** 12 hours	
Q20. 0015		**Q45.** 20%	
Q21. 1215		**Q46.** 62 prisoners	
Q22. 1330		**Q47.** 92 prisoners	
Q23. 10 hours		**Q48.** 63 prisoners	
Q24. Bus B		**Q49.** 56 prisoners	
Q25. 105		**Q50.** 84 prisoners	

Once you have checked your answers move on to the next mock exam.

CHAPTER 5
MOCK EXAM 4

During this next batch of sample test questions there are 40 questions. You have 20 minutes to complete the test. You are permitted to use a calculator.

Q1. There are 800 prisoners at HMP Rowenshaw and a total of 40 prison officers. What is the ratio of prisoners to prison officers?

Answer:

Q2. At HMP Rowenshaw 60% of prison officers apply for promotion. How many do not apply?

Answer:

Q3. A prison officer is required to search 25% of all visitors to HMP Rowenshaw. If there are 60 visitors, how many does he have to search?

Answer:

Q4. A prison officer can search six visitors in one hour. How many can he search in 6 hours?

Answer:

Q5. Compare the following two lists below. Write down the number of the line(s) where you identify a difference between the two lists.

LIST 1

1	Allardyce	23	Remand	Vegetarian
2	Bishop	22	Other	Vegetarian
3	Mitton	26	Life	Dairy free
4	Darby	29	Remand	Vegan
5	Hardy	33	Sex offender	Dairy free
6	Bendall	38	Other	Vegan
7	Billings	29	Remand	Dairy free
8	Brimstead	41	Other	Vegetarian

LIST 2

1	Allardyce	23	Remand	Vegetarian
2	Bishop	22	Remand	Vegetarian
3	Mitton	26	Other	Dairy free
4	Darby	29	Remand	Vegan
5	Hardy	33	Sex offender	Dairy free
6	Bendall	33	Other	Dairy free
7	Billings	29	Remand	Dairy free
8	Brimstead	41	Other	Vegan

Answer: [   ]

The following diagram represents prisoners serving at HMP Leyland and their different locations.

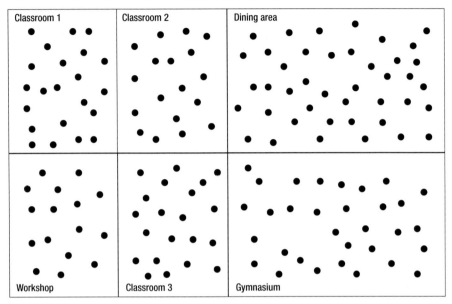

● = 1 prisoner

Q6. How many prisoners are there in the Dining area?

Answer:

Q7. How many prisoners are there in the Classrooms 1 and 2?

Answer:

Q8. Only a maximum of 15 prisoners are allowed in the workshop at any one time. How many prisoners need to leave in order to meet this requirement?

Answer:

Q9. If 50% of prisoners move from the Gymnasium to the Dining area, how many prisoners will there be left in the Gymnasium?

Answer:

You have been assigned to Blue wing at your first prison. List A is the official location of your prisoners. Prisoners can move freely around Blue wing providing they adhere to the following rules:

RULES:

1. Prisoners in cells A1, A2 and D2 are not allowed in cells A3, D3 or D4.

2. No more than 3 prisoners are allowed in one cell at any one time.

3. Prisoners are only allowed to be on their own in their own cell.

Your supervisory manager has asked you to check the locations of all your prisoners to ensure none of them is breaking the rules.

List A: Official cell locations

A1	D1
Miles, Johnson, Carter	Smithson, Hutchinson, Davies
A2	D2
Hudson, Button, Smith	Davis, Rogers
A3	D3
Clipstone, Moore, Price	Hodges, Cartwright, Benson
A4	D4
Jules, Kipp, Manson	Winters, Yore, Trott
A5	D5
French, Barker	Bromley, Wall

List B is the observations you find after your investigation.

List B: Your observations

A1	D1
Miles, Johnson, Clipstone	Smithson, Hutchinson
A2	D2
Hudson, Button, Smith	Davis, Rogers, French

A3	D3
Barker, Carter	Cartwright, Benson, Davies
A4	D4
Jules, Kipp, Manson	Winters, Yore, Trott
A5	D5
Moore, Price	Bromley

Q10. Who, if anyone, is missing?

Answer:

Q11. Who, if anyone, is contravening Rule 1?

Answer:

Q12. Who, if anyone, is contravening Rule 2?

Answer:

Q13. Who, if anyone, is contravening Rule 3?

Answer:

Q14. Compare the following two lists below. Write down the number of the line(s) where you identify a difference between the two lists.

List 1

10	7826542	21	Powell	Other
9	220847	20	Barker	Vegan
8	891724	34	Hall	Vegan
7	17346189	36	Maslow	Vegetarian
6	0002415	31	Mares	Dairy free
5	6175902	39	Harrow	Vegetarian
4	82789023	38	James	Dairy free
3	80745821	44	Hunter	Vegetarian

List 2

10	7816542	21	Powell	Other
9	220847	20	Baker	Vegan
8	891724	34	Hall	Vegan
7	17346189	36	Maslow	Vegetarian
6	002415	30	Mares	Dairy free
5	6175902	39	Harrow	Vegetarian
4	82789028	38	James	Dairy free
3	80745821	44	Hunter	Vegetarian

Answer:

You have been assigned to Blue wing at your first prison. List A is the official location of your prisoners. Prisoners can move freely around Blue wing providing they adhere to the following rules:

RULES:

1. Prisoners in cells A1, A4 and D2 are not allowed in cells A2, D3 or D5.

2. No more than 3 prisoners are allowed in one cell at any one time.

3. Prisoners are only allowed to be on their own in their own cell.

Your supervisory manager has asked you to check the locations of all your prisoners to ensure none of them is breaking the rules.

List A: Official cell locations

A1	D1
Powell, Stuart, Wood	Rimmer, Morris
A2	D2
Greystone, Parker	Johnson, Craig, Sutherland
A3	D3
Slidders, Fretten, Johns	Sumners, Lipton, Potter
A4	D4
Hatton	Comer, Cramer, Hart
A5	D5
Grey, Walters, Porter	Willers, Jenson, Field

List B is the observations you find after your investigation.

List B: Your observations

A1 Powell, Wood, Jenson	D1 Rimmer, Porter
A2 Greystone, Parker	D2 Johnson, Craig,
A3 Slidders, Fretten, Johns	D3 Sumners, Potter
A4 Comer	D4 Cramer, Hart, Hatton, Stuart
A5 Grey, Walters	D5 Willers , Field, Sutherland

Q15. Who, if anyone, is missing?

Answer:

Q16. Who, if anyone, is contravening Rule 1?

Answer:

Q17. Who, if anyone, is contravening Rule 2?

Answer:

Q18. Who, if anyone, is contravening Rule 3?

Answer:

Q19. A prison officer can search 7 visitors in one hour. How many can he search in 9 hours?

Answer:

Q20. In total there are 136 prisoners living on a wing of a prison and there are 17 prison officers on duty. What is the ratio of prisoners to prison officers?

Answer:

Q21. In total there are 288 prisoners living on a wing of a prison and there are 24 prison officers on duty. What is the ratio of prisoners to prison officers?

Answer:

Q22. It takes a prison officer 12 minutes to complete one prisoner report sheet. How many can she complete in 5 hours?

Answer:

Q23. At HMP Throwley there are 90 prison officers. If 30% of prison officers apply for promotion, how many apply?

Answer:

Q24. There are 400 prisoners at HMP Clipton. Of these:

80 are below the age of 20;

160 are between the ages of 20 and 25;

260 are over the age of 25.

What percentage or prisoners at HMP Clipton are below the age of 20?

Answer:

Q25. There are 400 prisoners at HMP Clipton. Of these:

80 are below the age of 20;

160 are between the ages of 20 and 25;

260 are over the age of 25.

What percentage or prisoners at HMP Clipton are between the ages of 20 and 25?

Answer:

Q26. There are 400 prisoners at HMP Clipton. Of these:

80 are below the age of 20;

160 are between the ages of 20 and 25;

260 are over the age of 25.

If 20% of prisoners over the age of 25 leave HMP Clipton, how many prisoners will there be left over the age of 25?

Answer:

Q27. There are 500 prisoners at HMP Gorton. Of these:

30% are below the age of 20;

40% are between the ages of 20 and 25;

30% are over the age of 25.

How many prisoners at HMP Gorton are below the age of 20?

Answer:

Q28. There are 300 prisoners at HMP Wooton. Of these:

40% are below the age of 20;

40% are between the ages of 20 and 25;

20% are over the age of 25.

How many prisoners at HMP Wooton are between the ages of 20 and 25?

Answer:

Q29. At your first prison you have been asked to check a random 30% of prisoner mail. There are 160 letters in total. How many letters must you check?

Answer:

Q30. A prison officer is required to supervise prisoners in the gymnasium for 110 minutes. If he starts supervising at 19:00 hours, what time will he finish? (Use 24-hour clock)

Answer:

Q31. A prison officer is required to check a prisoner every 15 minutes. How many times must he check him in a 5-hour period?

Answer:

Q32. A prison officer is required to supervise prisoners in the gymnasium for 140 minutes. If she starts supervising at 11:20 hours, what time will she finish? (Use 24-hour clock)

Answer:

Q33. 90 visitors arrive at HMP Walston. You are required to search 40% of visitors. Each search takes 4 minutes to complete. How long will it take you to search 40% of visitors?

Answer:

Q34. 160 visitors arrive at HMP Grangemoor. You are required to search 40% of the visitors. Each search takes 4 minutes to complete. If you start searching at 14:10 hours, what time will you finish? (Use 24-hour clock)

Answer:

Q35. 150 visitors arrive at HMP Daleside. You are required to search 40% of the visitors. Each search takes 3 minutes to complete. If you start searching at 10:10 hours, what time will you finish? (Use 24-hour clock)

Answer: [   ]

You have been assigned to Green wing at your first prison. List A is the official location of your prisoners. Prisoners can move freely around Green wing providing they adhere to the following rules:

RULES:

1. Prisoners in cells A1, A2 and A3 are not allowed in cells D1, D2 or D3.

2. No more than 2 prisoners are allowed in cells A1, A4 or D1 at any one time.

3. Prisoners are only allowed to be on their own in their own cell.

Your supervisory manager has asked you to check the locations of all your prisoners to ensure none of them is breaking the rules.

List A: Official cell locations

A1	D1
Monk, Jarvis	Grimthorpe
A2	D2
Wentworth, Jackson, Smith	Willis, Wallis
A3	D3
Ahmed, Langley	Hatwell, Brown, Fredricks
A4	D4
Deverill, Scot	Fenton, Cedar
A5	D5
Attwell, Grimes	Leadbetter, Byron

List B is the observations you find after your investigation.

List B: *Your observations*

A1 Monk	D1 Grimthorpe, Jarvis
A2 Jackson, Smith	D2 Willis, Wallis, Wentworth
A3 Ahmed, Langley	D3 Brown
A4 Scott, Byron	D4 Hatwell
A5 Fredricks	D5 Leadbetter, Grimes, Attwell

Q36. Who, if anyone, is missing?

Answer:

Q37. Who, if anyone, is contravening Rule 1?

Answer:

Q38. Who, if anyone, is contravening Rule 2?

Answer:

Q39. Who, if anyone, is contravening Rule 3?

Answer:

Q40. 360 people apply to become a prison officer. Of this number, 55% are male and 45% are female. How many male applicants are there?

Answer:

Now check your answers with the ones that follow before moving on to the next section of the guide..

ANSWERS TO MOCK EXAM 4

Q1. 20:1

Q2. 16

Q3. 15

Q4. 36

Q5. Lines 2, 3, 6 and 8

Q6. 42

Q7. 40

Q8. 1

Q9. 16

Q10. Hodges and Wall

Q11. Carter

Q12. Nobody

Q13. Bromley

Q14. 10, 9, 6 and 4

Q15. Morris and Lipton

Q16. Sutherland

Q17. Stuart

Q18. Comer

Q19. 63 searches

Q20. 8:1

Q21. 12:1

Q22. 25 reports

Q23. 27 prison officers

Q24. 20%

Q25. 40%

Q26. 208 prisoners

Q27. 150 prisoners

Q28. 120 prisoners

Q29. 48 letters

Q30. 2050 hours

Q31. 20 checks

Q32. 1340 hours

Q33. 144 minutes or 2 hours and 24 minutes

Q34. 1826 hours

Q35. 1310 hours

Q36. Deverill, Fenton and Cedar

Q37. Jarvis and Wentworth

Q38. Nobody

Q39. Hatwell and Fredricks

Q40. 198

Once you have checked your answers move on to the next section of the guide.

CHAPTER 6
RECALLING VISUAL INFORMATION TEST

During this test, which forms part of the Recruitment Assessment Day, you will be shown a colour photograph of a prison scene for three minutes. The photograph is then removed and you will be asked a number of questions about what you saw. Note taking is not permitted on this exercise.

I have found that one of the most effective ways to prepare for this test is to carry out exercises that improve your memory. There are a number of products on the market that will serve this purpose such as Brain Trainer.

The key to storing visual information into your memory is concentration; unless you focus on information intently, it will go away and you won't be able to recall it. This is why teachers are always nagging students to pay attention! You need to focus your mind intently on the scene presented in front of you for three minutes solid, taking in all that you see. Let's assume that you are presented with an image of two prisoners in a prison cell. Things you would focus on might include:

> What are the prisoners doing? Are they sitting down, standing or interacting in a certain way?

> What clothes are the prisoners wearing and what colour are their clothes/shoes?

> Are there any objects in the cell such as a television, sink, cups etc?

> What's on the walls of the prison cell?

> Are there any numbers in the image that you may be asked to recall?

TIPS FOR PREPARING FOR THE RECALLING VISUAL INFORMATION TEST

> The fact that you are being asked to memorise 'visual' information is a benefit. It is far easier to remember visual items, than items that are in written format. In the build-up to your assessment read newspaper articles for three minutes and then get a friend to ask you questions based on the content.

> Pick a photograph from a magazine. Study it for three minutes before getting a friend to ask you questions about the image.

> Consider using a brain-training game or resource. These are fun and they can go a long way to improving your memory ability.

On the following pages I have provided you with a number of memory tests that will go a long way to helping you improve your memory.

SAMPLE MEMORY TEST 1

Study the following words for three minutes only. Once the three minutes are complete, turn the page and answer the questions without referring back to words.

Mouse	Bicycle	Trumpet	Motorcar
Hate	Brick	Bark	Snake
Help	Waterfall	Lion	Trombone
Drums	Train	Oboe	River
Dog	Lake	Crow	Guitar

SAMPLE MEMORY TEST 1 QUESTIONS

Q1. How many words are there in total?

Answer: [ ]

Q2. How many animals are there?

Answer: [ ]

Q3. How many objects have wheels?

Answer: [ ]

Q4. How many musical instruments are there?

Answer: [ ]

Once you have checked through your answers on page 77, move on to sample memory test 2.

SAMPLE MEMORY TEST 2

Study the following words for three minutes only. Once the three minutes are complete, turn the page and answer the questions without referring back to words.

White	Dog	Football	Boxing
Badminton	Brick	Cricket	Cat
Fish	Rugby	Mouse	Trombone
Rat	Brown	Oboe	Tennis
Yellow	Eagle	Crow	Black

SAMPLE MEMORY TEST 2 QUESTIONS

Q1. How many colours are there in total?

Answer: [   ]

Q2. How many different types of sports are there?

Answer: [   ]

Q3. How many animals are there?

Answer: [   ]

Q4. How many three-letter words are there?

Answer: [   ]

Once you have checked through your answers on page 77, move on to sample memory test 3.

SAMPLE MEMORY TEST 3

Study the following words for three minutes only. Once the three minutes are complete, turn the page and answer the questions without referring back to words.

Brook	Crate	Bite	Boxing
Badminton	Brick	Bonus	Carpet
Broom	Cringe	Yacht	Yellow
Car	Bellow	Colour	Yes
Boots	Yard	Crow	Black

SAMPLE MEMORY TEST 3 QUESTIONS

Q1. How many words begin with the letter Y?

Answer: [   ]

Q2. How many words begin with the letter B?

Answer: [   ]

Q3. How many words begin with the letter C?

Answer: [   ]

Q4. How many three-letter words are there?

Answer: [   ]

Once you have checked through your answers on page 77, move on to sample memory test 4.

SAMPLE MEMORY TEST 4

Study the following shapes for three minutes only. Once the three minutes are complete, turn the page and answer the questions without referring back to shapes.

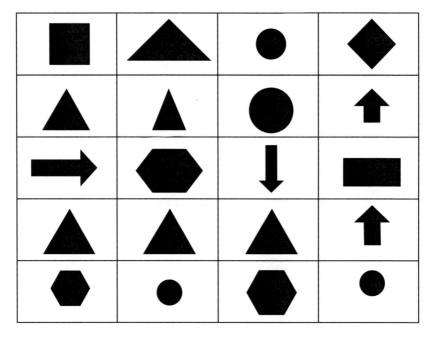

SAMPLE MEMORY TEST 4 QUESTIONS

Q1. How many shapes are there in total?

Answer:

Q2. How many four sided shapes are there?

Answer:

Q3. How many arrows point to the left?

Answer:

Q4. How many triangles are there?

Answer:

Once you have checked through your answers on page 77, move on to sample memory test 5.

SAMPLE MEMORY TEST 5

Study the following shapes for three minutes only. Once the three minutes are complete, turn the page and answer the questions without referring back to shapes.

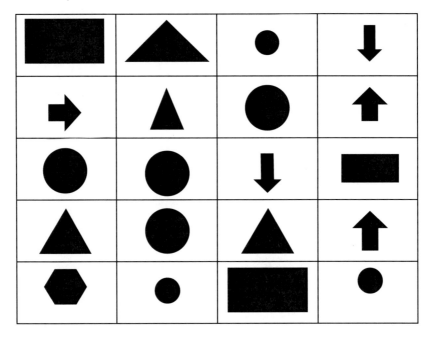

SAMPLE MEMORY TEST 5 QUESTIONS

Q1. How many 7 sided shapes are there?

Answer:

Q2. How many arrows are pointing downwards?

Answer:

Q3. How many 6 sided shapes are there?

Answer:

Q4. How many triangles are there?

Answer:

Once you have checked through your answers on page 77, move on to sample memory test 6.

SAMPLE MEMORY TEST 6

Study the following words and shapes for three minutes only. Once the three minutes are complete, turn the page and answer the questions without referring back to words or shapes.

Pink	Coat	Bin	Socks
⬡ (octagon)	← (left arrow)	▬ (small rectangle)	▽ (trapezoid)
Apple	Cot	Rum	Green
→ (right arrow)	← (left arrow)	⬡ (octagon)	↑ (up arrow)
Chisel	Trousers	Red	Pear

SAMPLE MEMORY TEST 6 QUESTIONS

Q1. How many shapes are there in total?

Answer: [   ]

Q2. How many items of clothing are there?

Answer: [   ]

Q3. How many arrows point to the left?

Answer: [   ]

Q4. How many three-letter words are there?

Answer: [   ]

ANSWERS TO SAMPLE MEMORY TESTS

TEST 1 ANSWERS

Q1. 20

Q2. 5

Q3. 3

Q4. 5

TEST 2 ANSWERS

Q1. 4

Q2. 6

Q3. 7

Q4. 3

TEST 3 ANSWERS

Q1. 4

Q2. 10

Q3. 6

Q4. 2

TEST 4 ANSWERS

Q1. 20

Q2. 3

Q3. 0

Q4. 6

TEST 5 ANSWERS

Q1. 5

Q2. 2

Q3. 1

Q4. 3

TEST 6 ANSWERS

Q1. 8

Q2. 3

Q3. 2

Q4. 4

CHAPTER 7
READING COMPREHENSION TESTS

During the Recruitment Assessment Day you will be required to carry out a reading comprehension exercise. Basically, you'll need to read text that has been taken from a standard Prison Service source. This could be either from the internet (Prison Service website), Prison Service Orders or manuals.

Whilst you do not need to carry out any pre-assessment preparation for this exercise, you can improve your ability in this test by:

1. Visiting and reading the Prison Service website at:
   www.hmprisonservice.gov.uk
   Read the information on the website and learn as much as possible about the role of a Prison Officer and also the Prison Service.

2. Take the time to read some of the more important Prison Service Orders relevant to the role of a Prison Officer.

On the following page I have provided you with a sample reading comprehension exercise.

Study the passage for 5 minutes only before answering the questions on the next page. You are not permitted to take notes and you are not permitted to refer back to the passage once the 5 minutes are complete.

SAMPLE READING COMPREHENSION EXERCISE 1

Prison Industries

Prison Industries is a Headquarters Unit within the NOMS Employment, Skills and Services Group that provides an overall strategic and policy framework for prison industries. The Statement of Purpose is:

"The aim of the Prison Industries is to occupy prisoners in out of cell activity and wherever possible to help them gain skills, qualifications and work experience to improve their employment prospects upon release. The management of industries must weigh the true costs and benefits to the organisation and constantly strive for greater efficiency in providing developmental opportunities for prisoners."

Prisons provide prisoners with the chance to learn the skills they need to get a job upon release. Employment is known to be a key factor in helping to reduce re-offending. The Government's aim therefore is to provide more prisoners with the skills and motivation to turn away from crime, improve their employability, and become productive members of society.

Prison Industries provides a supporting role to public sector prison establishments, for the management of their industrial workshops. It facilitates and coordinates the in-house production and supply of essential clothing and goods for internal consumption, providing essential employment for prisoners and opportunities for them to gain skills, qualifications and work experience to improve their employability prospects upon release.

SAMPLE READING COMPREHENSION EXERCISE 1

Q1. The aim of the Prison Industries is to occupy prisoners in what?

Answer:

Q2. Prison Industries facilitates and coordinates the in-house production and supply of essential what for internal consumption?

Answer:

Q3. Prisons provide prisoners with the chance to learn what?

Answer:

Q4. The Statement of Purpose states that the management of industries must weigh the true costs and benefits to the organisation and constantly strive for greater efficiency in providing developmental opportunities for whom?

Answer:

Now that you have completed reading comprehension exercise 1, move on to exercise 2. Check answers on page 84.

SAMPLE READING COMPREHENSION EXERCISE 2

Study the passage for 5 minutes only before answering the questions on the next page. You are not permitted to take notes and you are not permitted to refer back to the passage once the 5 minutes are complete

Prison Industries

There are over 300 workshops employing around 10,000 prisoners each week day in a range of disciplines including producing goods for the internal market, including complex and challenging production tasks such as clothing, window frames, woodwork, office furniture manufacturing, plastic injection moulding, printing, light engineering and laundries.

Aside from producing a wide range of goods and services for prisons Prison Industry workshops also provide goods for consumption within the wider National Offender Management Service (NOMS) and Ministry of Justice (MoJ) including office furniture and printing services. In summary, the main purpose of providing work for prisoners whilst in custody is therefore to:

- provide goods and services as efficiently and effectively as possible – this reduces the cost of imprisonment, has an element of restitution and promotes the idea of active regimes rather than having prisoners unoccupied;

- aid good order and control by employing significant numbers of prisoners;

- aid resettlement through skills and qualifications; and where possible

- raise a financial contribution to offset the high cost of imprisonment.

Work is also undertaken for commercial customers ranging from simple tasks such as filling mail-shot envelopes to assembling electrical components – this is known as 'contract services' work.

SAMPLE READING COMPREHENSION EXERCISE 2

Q1. There are over 300 workshops employing around how many prisoners each week?

Answer:

Q2. Work is also undertaken for commercial customers ranging from simple tasks such as filling mail-shot envelopes to assembling electrical components – this is known as what type of work.

Answer:

Q3. Aside from producing a wide range of goods and services for prisons Prison Industry workshops also provide goods for consumption within the wider National Offender Management Service (NOMS) and Ministry of Justice (MoJ) including office furniture and what?

Answer:

Q4. In summary, the main purpose of providing work for prisoners whilst in custody is therefore to aid good order and control by doing what?

Answer:

SAMPLE READING COMPREHENSION TEST ANSWERS

EXERCISE 1

Q1. Out of cell activity and wherever possible to help them gain skills, qualifications and work experience to improve their employment prospects upon release.

Q2. Clothing and goods.

Q3. The skills they need to get a job upon release.

Q4. Prisoners.

EXERCISE 2

Q1. 10,000 prisoners.

Q2. Contract services.

Q3. Printing services.

Q4. Employing significant numbers of prisoners.

A FEW FINAL WORDS

You have now reached the end of the guide and no doubt you will be ready to start preparing even further for the prison officer selection process. Just before you go off and start on your preparation, consider the following.

The majority of candidates who pass the selection process have a number of common attributes. These are as follows:

1. They believe in themselves.

The first factor is self-belief. Regardless of what anyone tells you, you can become a Prison Officer. Just like any job of this nature, you have to be prepared to work hard in order to be successful. Make sure you have the self-belief to pass the selection process and fill your mind with positive thoughts.

2. They prepare fully.

The second factor is preparation. Those people who achieve in life prepare fully for every eventuality and that is what you must do when you apply to become a Prison Officer. Work very hard and especially concentrate on your weak areas.

3. They persevere.

Perseverance is a fantastic word. Everybody comes across obstacles or setbacks in their life, but it is what you do about those setbacks that is important. If you fail at something, then ask yourself 'why' you have failed. This will allow you to improve for next time and if you keep improving and trying, success will eventually follow. Apply this same method of thinking when you apply to become a Prison Officer.

4. They are self-motivated.

How much do you want this job? Do you want it, or do you really want it?

When you apply to join the Prison Service you should want it more than anything in the world. Your levels of self-motivation will shine through during the assessments. For the weeks and months leading up to the selection process, be motivated as best you can and always keep your fitness levels up as this will serve to increase your levels of motivation.

Work hard, stay focused and be what you want…

Richard McMunn

Richard McMunn

P.S Please visit my website **www.how2become.co.uk** for more information on how to become a prison officer.

Visit www.how2become.co.uk to find more titles and courses that will help you to pass the Prison Officer selection process, including:

- How to pass the Prison Officer Role-Play DVD.

- 1-Day Prison Officer training course.

- Online Prison Officer Selection Test.

- Psychometric testing books and CDs.

WWW.HOW2BECOME.CO.UK